Stormy Seas - The Remedy © 2023 Vicki Watson

Presentation by *BookLeaf Publishing*

Web: www.bookleafpub.com

E-mail: info@bookleafpub.com

ISBN: 9789358316544

First edition 2023

Stormy Seas - The Remedy

Vicki Watson

BookLeaf
Publishing
India | USA | UK

Gail Watson - my mum. The Dancing Queen forever dancing in the sky with the stars xx

ACKNOWLEDGEMENT

The Remedy Cafe, Ayr Seafront, for their inspiration.
My friends and family in life who have helped get me through the hardest days. Thank you.

PREFACE

The hope to inspire, discover and learn your own remedies to be used along the journey of life. Sometimes in life it is helpful to know that many other people are going through difficult times too, or have done so.

We often think "is it just me?". Inevitably, we all experience some form of distress, grief and loss. The poems aim to cover various aspects of this and the associated array of emotions. Loss of; relationships, friendship, sense of self, loved ones - to name a few.

To know along with the duller days, there will always be sunnier days ahead. We just have to be patient. Even though it may not seem it at the time, we can always find solutions in the storm.

Stormy Seas - The Remedy.

I could have stayed in bed today, under the safe
covers, but instead I went a walk.

I could have hid away again, comfy in the house,
but instead I phoned you for a talk.

I could have let things get to me, in my head it
all stacks up. Overwhelmed, all too much, but
instead I wrote a list of where to start.
I know this will help my heart.

I could have lost my rag again and in a mood I'd
go, but instead I took a deep breath and
paused-and tried to just go with the flow.

I could have tried to keep control by frantically
feeling I should be doing something productive.
Instead while out, I put my feet up and just let
life do it's thing around me for a change.

I could have sat and stared into space wondering
why life is harsh at times. Instead I remembered
the way I feel today is just a drop in the ocean- a
snapshot- and there's times I've felt better soon
after. I know I WILL feel better soon.

Like the waves, I'll just wait for it to pass, but it's good to think of remedies to help it along a wee bit faster.

Remedies for the could and should haves, all too harsh on myself at times. This is why I'm writing these rhymes, a remedy you see, something that helps me.

A wee hot chocolate, a cheeky wee cake from "The Remedy Cafe". A wee treat to myself, helps with the healing I say.

I sat and looked at the crashing waves and my sadness began to slowly fade. With each wave a worry joined it back out to sea. Thank goodness it left me.

The sun kept peeking behind the clouds, now and then, reminding that if we wait long enough there can be rays of much needed light.

A reminder that things can change as quickly as it happened. If we are patient- the stormy seas can pass.

As I've sat here on this wall, one thing has become clear, all these other people out here walking around, maybe they feel the same way, or thinking about the ones they miss so dear. Or maybe they just popped out for fresh air. Either way - this has been their remedy. Their drop in the ocean of what makes them feel better. Everyone I've passed has appeared happier for being out, even though the wind has blown them about!

It's as if the sea is a healer, for life can be an awful dealer. People smiling back at me as they turn to watch the sea with glee.

So no matter how stormy and wild the sea may look or seem, it has it's own healing properties - and in a matter of hours can return itself to calmer waters again.

Even the sea knows it can be it's own remedy.

Missing You

"Time will heal ", but will it really?
Not even a wee bit, not even nearly.

The more days that pass, the months, and years.
Still won't ease the volume of my tears.

One minute I'm fine, then out of the blue,
A sad pang, my heart thinks of you.

A simple thing- like a day of cheer,
I know you'd love this, I wish you were here.

What can I do when you're so far,
I can't just visit you in my car.

One thing is true, is my memories of you that
will get me through.

I know I love you, that's all I can say. I'll bide
my time, and see you again one day.

Frazzled

It's like a ticking clock in my head, when all I
want to do is go to my bed.
All the tasks I know I have to do, it feels like
millions but I know it's really only a few.

I often feel useless that I can't keep on top,
all lifes stresses, the bills, the big shop.

What's this now, my MOT is due, just when I
thought I had nothing left to do.

Where to start - I know I'll have to soon, no use
taking to bed or sitting all day in my room. But
how do you get the notion to pick yourself up, to
make that start, do that first part.

I remembered something that helped me before -
I'll write it all down - a list for my chores.
This way it's not all building up in my head,
down on paper I'll work through it instead.

That's the first task done, it was actually quite
fun. Not as hard as I thought, now on to the
second one.

Another one ticked off the list - I've got this -
this life thing - well maybe only for today!
But I know I can do it and this I'll remember, as
I often feel quite sluggish come the month of
December.

So I'll try not to be too hard on myself as I
navigate this lifes endless 'to do list'. Give
myself a break, I'm only one person. I'll pull
myself once again through this busy mist.

A Rose

Tall and elegant, motionless. Nothing sways it
except the wind, because it's so calm and cool.

A tear or a frown, it makes us all smile when we
are down, because it is so happy and cheerful.

It smells so sweet, the soft purple and pink
petals, sitting at the bottom of the garden.

To touch, it is sharp, because of the thorns,
to see, a delight because it is bright.

Mum, just like a rose you were so calm and
cool, cheerful and bright. You made everyone's
day a little happier.

You don't have thorns and you don't sit at the
bottom of the garden.
The place you are is the bottom of my heart,
because I love you mum!

19/08/02.
For Mum.

Torn

I wish it was something I knew the answer to,
Black or white?,
Tea or coffee?,
Rain or sunshine?
Dark or light?

One minute I know the answer and I'm certain I
know what to do,
but my tender heart often gets pulled back, along
that familiar, comfortable, warm path.

I wish someone would tell me exactly what to
do, everyone I've relayed my feelings to say "it's
really up to you".

Without a doubt the hardest decision I've ever
had to make to date,
to walk away from this, I know,
will help me learn and grow.

It's good to move on, sometimes stagnant we can
remain,
but unhappy that life would be, just going with
the motions,
just getting soaked in the gloomy rain.

Onwards toward some sunshine, I know we'll still be friends, better apart now than together, we'll still get each other through all sorts of weather.

A Sign

Hello wee robin, sitting on the tree,
what's brought you here today, just to see me?

I saw a wee white feather today,
falling from the sky,
I wondered if it was a gift from you,
a tear fell from my eye.

Was it just coincidence?,
Was it really for me?,
A sign from you just to tell me true,
of course "I love you too".

I've been asking you to just let me know,
and telling you that I miss you so,
Are you OK? Can you hear me?,
and did you really have to go?

Just a wee thing for me then I'll know,
can you hear my prayers? - up all those stairs -
in heaven? - so far away.

A robin, a feather, or anything really, not much I
ask to help with my healing.

Just a wee token - all I need you see - a sign that
says -
"Hello there, it's me".

Running Late

How on earth has this happened again?,
 a minute ago it was only 20 past 10!

I can't believe again I'm running late,
in a flap, in a panic, in a state.

It's really getting quite out of hand,
but the clock just seems to go like quicksand.

I do have a watch and I set an alarm,
doesn't matter now, I'll try to stay calm.

Even my friends, they trick me you see,
2 instead of 3 - so on time I'll be!

I really have tried every trick in the book, but
still I turn up dishevelled- quite a look!

If ever a prize for running late,
it's a skill at which I'm really quite great!

So if ever we do have plans made,
just know I tried to make the grade!

I am truly sorry but this is just me,
on time I'll likely never be.

Imagined Life

When I'm cooking the dinner, or putting the
shopping away,
I often hope that in you'll walk, and for a cuppa
you'll stay.

In the shops, unsure I browse,
the shoes, that top - oh that pattern so loud!
I often hope that in you'll walk,
"Aye hen, that one, that colour will pop".

I would phone you up just to chat,
about the antics of my new cat.
Or vent to you about my work,
or just whenever I felt stuck.

How I long to hear you say,
"Hello hen it's me",
"my new hairdo, wait till you see".

I often hope that in my house you'll visit,
"Just me to see you - and my grandbabies- now
there's two?!".

The hardest part of losing you, is all these things
we don't get to do.

About these things I can still dream,
when I think of you my smile will beam.

The Violet Light

Have you ever missed someone before they're
gone?
An odd thought to think,
I've been hoping I've been wrong.

Your bright light once lit my path,
you often helped me in my dark.

We were supposed to be soulmates,
I thought it was true,
how can I ever live this life without you?

Your quirks, your smile - they're what got me
loving you all the while.
Not sure what to do now,
one day I'd hoped we'd make our vows.

You're still in my life but I'm grieving for you,
that violet light we had, that was our colour, our
hue.
Until one day the colour between us faded like a
mist,
Our souls, once entwined, undone. That's the
jist.

Maybe one day, I'll wake up and it's been a dream,
but for now I'll just accept,
it's not what it seemed.

Letter to my granny

"Are you not coming outside to sit in the sun?",
you'd say.
Sorry I'm too busy with this essay.

"Why don't you come and watch telly with
me?".
Sorry, I'm just getting ready to go out.

"Do you want to go into town with me?".
Do I have to?! I'd think, but agree.

I'd give absolutely anything right now to rewind
to all those moments - precious with you.
And I'd pause - and think - these years together,
we only have a few.

I'd have made more effort to look after you.
Bring you supper, make sure you were all tucked
in.
I'd do anything now to hear your laugh and see
your lovely grin.

I'm sorry for being selfish, and all wrapped up in
"me",
I didn't know what I know now,

the valuable lessons of gratitude, you see.

It's ironic that we need to go through these
lessons, to build our values and wisdom in life.
I just wish I knew it then,
I'm sorry if I ever caused you any strife.

So I hope you somehow get to see this letter,
and that you can forgive me Granny- I did not
think for the better.
A silly young girl, all Uni and friends,
But I'd walk the earth to see you again.

Night night.
See you in the morning.
Love you.
X

Starry Sky

Shining bright way up high,
a blanket of stars in the deep black abyss.
They twinkle, shimmer and pierce like
diamonds,
and the clouds appear to give them a kiss.

The space so vast and stars abundant,
surely at least one will hear my thoughts, or
grant my wish.

Please take these dark thoughts and with your
illuminating rays they'll diminish,
and return me pure love, answers or advice.
I'll accept each with gratitude, and my heavy
woes will finish.

Always an answer does the sky have,
even just to look at - the distraction - a life raft.

So any time time you're lost and you need a
helping hand,
remember you're never lonely, with all these
stars in the land.

Dream

I thought I heard your voice today, I guess it wasn't true.
In my head I hoped it was, as I've got a lot to say to you.

I heard a funny story today, I thought - wait till I tell you.
Then that pang - back with a bang -
I can't - and with sorrow my heart sang.

I went to call your name today, but remembered about you,
you had to go, we don't know why,
these questions I have a few.

Is this real?
Is this my life?
Is this how I'm supposed to feel?

What will we do now, without you?
These feelings of anger and sadness they brew.

So when I go to sleep, a photo of you I'll keep.
I'll talk to you and tell you it all, but oh how I'd do anything for one last call.

A prayer to the sky with stars a-few,
that when I go to sleep,
I hope I'll dream of you.

Chapters

Remember that girl? From years ago?
30, 21 ...and then back to the school years, they
were fun.
Being young - no cares, responsibilities.
Where did it all go?

She would go and do her learning, fun with Uni
friends, and work at the weekends.
Nights out galore,
she was always heading out the door!

Never off the dance floor, not wanting the night
to end, now there's not a party in sight,
and it's the garden or housework she'll tend.

She'd head out for dinners a-plenty, and parties
she adored.
Trips away a weekend to stay, with a hangover,
she'd often be floored!

No hangovers now that she's a mummy, her
babies are too precious to leave, that mum guilt
too, when you do go out to enjoy 'just you'.

She misses 'the old chapters' of her life, they
didn't seem to have as much strife.
 But she's reminded daily of all she has now -
lucky she is, she'll often ask how.

You can't skip chapters,
she would never have got here without all those
years, tears and fears.
It's all learning she'll say - part of life. It's how
we grow.
Regrets a few,
of course, we're human - we do.

Looking forward to the next chapter, wonder
what's in store....
Embracing her new 'you' , and that girl you
knew...she's happy too.

Little You

From the first time we saw the "positive",
we couldn't quite believe it was true,
blessed with a little you.

From the first conversations about you,
Pink or blue...names - we had a good few.
We loved you - little you.

Getting used to you being in my tummy,
the nausea in the morning- a reminder-
It was all to be worth it to be your mummy.

Thinking of clothes, socks for your little toes,
wondering about the shape of your little nose.
We couldn't wait to plan for you.

A long 12 weeks, it seemed to drag in,
desperate to see you on the screen.
And mum and dad's smiles, they would beam.

The day came and we anxiously waited, looking
forward to finally seeing you.
The cold jelly on my belly, swirling round with
the scanner machine.

"How far along do you think you are?".
"12 weeks", my sure response.
"Could you be sooner?", she quietly asked.
"No" why ask that, I thought.
"We are not seeing what we'd expect to see at
this stage " her voice - after a pause.

A heart wrenching overwhelm of tears
consumed, and soon my cries filled the whole
room.
I knew something was wrong then and there, but
why me? Why now? It didn't seem fair!

The shock, my thoughts wandered, as to why
this had happened.
Was it me? Something I'd done?
"I've had the odd coffee" I tried to blame myself.
"Have I done this?".
"No, not at all" , her voiced seemed to fade
away.

Through to another room to speak to a doctor:
my body didn't let me know. I thought you
continued to grow.

Still searching for answers for "why". Sadly no
concrete explanation could be given,
only that this can be common.

Sobbing all the while, quietly listening, anxiety
driven.

" Come back in a week to see if there's growth".
We somehow knew there wouldn't be.
Confirmed heartbreak for us both.

You're not lost to us, you're always on our
minds.
We made you with love and with that the three
of us binds.

Mummy and Daddy loved you Little You,
We still very much do.

Till we meet again.
XX

Hello again

No goodbyes, not for me either.
So if I say hello again, will that be OK?

Seems like yesterday you asked me "you alright
hen? ".
"I'm fine....are you?".
"Aye I'm fine", you replied shakily.

Then you were gone.

Then I knew I had to be strong.
If only I'd have known that'd be the last time
we'd talk.
Never again I'd get to join you on a walk.

Or a wander around the town for hours a-few, or
for a wee lunch.
Or you'd take me on a visit, to the many friends
you knew.

What would I have said when saying goodbye?
I say it everytime I close my eyes.

Thanks for being 'my' mum, and for all that you
did. And thanks for our wee chats and laughs
when I was a kid.

Instead of closing my eyes now, I'll just look to
the skies,
No need for goodbyes....
It's "Hello again".

Stages of grief - Denial

I tried to sit with the grief and it said,
go away, not today,
I won't let you in my head.

I don't want to believe it,
it doesn't seem fair.
Only yesterday I saw you skipping down the
stairs.

So I'll tell myself it's not quite true.
Someone will tell me there's been a mistake.
To protect myself I keep telling my head lies.
My heart knows you really had to go,
and this certainly isn't fake.

My head will catch up with my heart, perhaps
very soon,
Until then - my new friend Denial,
It's me and you till noon.

Stages of grief- Bargaining.

So you're telling me my loved one has gone?
Are you sure?
Did you double check.....
Further tests? Did they work?

I sent up prayers begging for it to be a joke,
that if you sent her back to me my whole life, I'd
never smoke.

I promise I'll be a better person, if this one I can
keep,
but I know deep down the truth....I'm trying to
delay....pretend.

I'm not ready for this to be the end.

Stages of grief- Anger

I met with anger today, when I saw them
together in the shop.
And then I heard the girl say...
"mum, let's shop till we drop!".

My face must have been scarlet red,
with pure rage...was there steam coming out my
ears?
The tears... surging upwards from the knot in my
tummy,
All I could think about was my "us" through the
years.

Why does she get to have her mum?
Why not me?
Have I done something wrong?
Is this some kind of karma?

Will this anger pass? I really hope it does.

So I can get on with the nice thoughts of us.

Stages of grief- Depression

Drop.
Drop.
Drop.
There another goes.
With each surge of missing you,
a bitter tear flows.

I'm engulfed with these waves, they don't seem
to leave.
Soaring up high,
Then they take a
dive.

Been in the same clothes for two days now,
I just want life to be back to normal,
but I just don't know how.

What even is 'normal' now?
You're gone. What is the point in going on...

What's this? ....another wave,
A nice memory this time... floats up to the sky.
It's these lovely snippets of memories of you,
that grasp me tightly and pull me through.

Stages of grief- Acceptance

Flowers at your graveside, and a wee tidy.
I've been coming here more often now,
I finally feel ready.

Feelings of sadness, anger, denial and
resentment, they have drifted away.
Under no illusion they may visit my mind again
some days.

But for now I'm happy in my peace.
It's taken a long journey to get here.
The light I never thought I'd see, in the smallest
of everyday things....
...have helped give me such a release.

Time to accept.
You're no longer here.
And I'm not to blame.
No time or distance will extinguish our flame.

Time to heal now.
Learn from this pain.
Time to grow and move forward.
And dance happily right into the rain.

The day I met you again

I've been all round about,
Up and down.
Soaring way up high, crashing down low, with
this cycle of grief.

I'm happy to think of you,
then I'm in disbelief.

When I turn this corner, will I bump into you?
My phone rang earlier, I wondered if it was you?
Of course not- my head says.
Please just once...my heart whispers.

Cosy on the couch now, all curled up. My eyes
slowly closing...dosing...to dreamland I drift.
Into a hazy wonderland, soft clouds, golden
light.
Then someone took me by the hand...

Oh my goodness...can it be? ...is it really you?
It is!
It's you!
I know the outline of your face,
your every detail I can trace.

A great big cuddle, I just throw my arms round
you. This cuddle I've been waiting for...forever
it's true.

But wait...why am I here with you? Have you
come to take me too?

Not at all, you say softly,
It's only a wee visit, in your dream - it's been so
exquisite.
You needed that cuddle, I know, I've seen.
That feather- you missed it.
Our song on the radio - you couldn't hear either.
These signs you asked for - your tears have been
drowning out.
So I had to do something and do it loud!
Finally I reached you, to let you know,
It's never been goodbye.
It's always hello.

Milton Keynes UK
Ingram Content Group UK Ltd.
UKHW050026250324
439966UK00014BA/963